40 Weight Loss Recipes for a Busy Lifestyle:

The Solution to Dealing with Fat

By

Joseph Correa

Certified Sports Nutritionist

COPYRIGHT

© 2016 Finibi Inc

All rights reserved

Reproduction or translation of any part of this work beyond that permitted by section 107 or 108 of the 1976 United States Copyright Act without the permission of the copyright owner is unlawful.

This publication is designed to provide accurate and authoritative information in regard to the subject matter covered. It is sold with the understanding that neither the author nor the publisher is engaged in rendering medical advice. If medical advice or assistance is needed, consult with a doctor. This book is considered a guide and should not be used in any way detrimental to your health. Consult with a physician before starting this nutritional plan to make sure it's right for you.

ACKNOWLEDGEMENTS

The realization and success of this book could not have been possible without the motivation and support of my entire family.

40 Weight Loss Recipes for a Busy Lifestyle:

The Solution to Dealing with Fat

By

Joseph Correa

Certified Sports Nutritionist

CONTENTS

Copyright

Acknowledgements

About The Author

Introduction

Calendar

40 Weight Loss Recipes for a Busy Lifestyle: The Solution to Dealing with Fat

Other Great Titles by This Author

ABOUT THE AUTHOR

As a certified sports nutritionist, I honestly believe in the positive effects that proper nutrition can have over the body and mind. My knowledge and experience has helped me live healthier throughout the years and which I have shared with family and friends. The more you know about eating and drinking healthier, the sooner you will want to change your life and eating habits.

Nutrition is a key part in the process of being healthy and living longer so get started today.

INTRODUCTION

40 Weight Loss Recipes for a Busy Lifestyle will help you lose weight naturally and efficiently. Knowing what to eat and when will make all the difference in the world. If you haven't been successful in the past with losing that unwanted fat, now is your chance to make that change. Read this book and start living the life you deserve. The calendar and meal recipes are easy to follow and understand.

Being too busy to eat right can sometimes become a problem and that's why this book will save you time and help nourish your body to achieve the goals you want.

This book will help you to:

-Lose weight fast by eating delicious meals.

-Have more energy.

-Naturally accelerate Your Metabolism to become thinner.

-Improve your digestive system.

Joseph Correa is a certified sports nutritionist and a professional athlete.

WEIGHT LOSS CALENDAR

Week 1

Day 1:

Fruit and Nuts Yogurt

Egg Drop Soup with Chicken and Noodles

Mushroom Pilaf with Lemon

Day 2:

Egg and Veggie Breakfast Bakes

Turkey Stir Fry

Stuffed Eggplant

Day 3:

Breakfast Guacamole

Lemmon-rubbed Barbecued Salmon

Orange, Walnut and Blue Cheese Salad

Day 4:

Fitness Smoothie

Chicken and Corn Salad

Veggie Red Curry

Day 5:

Banana Oatmeal Pancakes

Tangy Trout

Stuffed Zucchinis

Day 6:

Tuna on Toast

Garlic Beef

Fruit Salad

Day 7:

Bacon and Brie Omelette with Salad

Rice and Tomato Soup

Smoked Trout with Beetroot, Fennel and Apple Salad

Week 2

Day 1:

Berry Smoothie

40 Weight Loss Recipes for a Busy Lifestyle

Lemon Spaghetti with Broccoli and Tuna

Devilled Mushrooms

Day 2:

Spring Onion and Turkey Wraps

Chicken with Mushrooms

Mexican Rice and Bean Salad

Day 3:

Poached Eggs with Smoked Salmon and Spinach

Bean and Pepper Chili

Thai Vegetable and Coconut Milk Broth

Day 4:

Hummus with Pita Bread and Vegetables

Grilled Fish with Moroccan Spiced Tomatoes

Lentil, Carrot and Orange Soup

Day 5:

Oatmeal with Apples and Raisins

Spicy Seafood Stew

Chickpeas and Spinach Curry

Day 6:

Feta and Semi-dried Tomato Omelette

Spinach and Dates Stuffed Chicken

Roasted Carrots with Pomegranate and Blue Cheese

Day 7:

Fruit and Nuts Yogurt

Prawn Curry

Mexican Rice and Bean Salad

Week 3

Day 1:

Bacon and Brie Omelette with Salad

Bean and Pepper Chili

Tangy Trout

Day 2:

Fitness Smoothie

Garlic Beef

Stuffed Eggplant

Day 3:

Breakfast Guacamole

Turkey Stir Fry

Fruit Salad

Day 4:

Egg and Veggie Breakfast Bakes

Lemon-rubbed Barbecued Salmon

Veggie Red Curry

Day 5:

Banana Oatmeal Pancakes

Egg Drop Soup with Chicken and Noodles

Smoked Trout with Beetroot, Fennel and Apple Salad

Day 6:

Tuna on Toast

Rice and Tomato Soup

Stuffed Zucchinis

Day 7:

Berry Smoothie

Chicken and Corn Salad

Orange, Walnut and Blue Cheese Dressing

Week 4

Day 1:

Oatmeal with Apples and Raisins

Lemon Spaghetti with Broccoli and Tuna

Lentil, Carrot and Orange Soup

Day 2:

Poached Eggs with Smoked Salmon and Spinach

Chicken with Mushrooms

Chickpeas and Spinach Curry

Day 3:

Spring Onion and Turkey Wraps

Spicy seafood Stew

Roasted Carrots with Pomegranate and Blue Cheese

Day 4:

Feta and Semi-dried Tomato Omelette

Bean and Pepper Chili

Fruit Salad

Day 5:

Hummus with Pita Bread and Vegetables

Prawn Curry

Mexican Rice and Bean Salad

Day 6:

Fruit and Nuts Yogurt

Spinach and Dates Stuffed Chicken

Thai Vegetable and Coconut Broth

Day 7:

Breakfast Guacamole

Tangy trout

Stuffed Eggplant

2 extra days for a full month:

Day 1:

Fitness Smoothie

Chicken and Corn Salad

Orange, Walnut and Blue Cheese Salad

Day 2:

Tuna on Toast

Turkey Stir Fry

Veggie Red Curry

WEIGHT LOSS RECIPES

BREAKFAST

1. Feta and Semi-dried Tomato Omelette

A really quick, simple, low calorie recipe that will give your day the kick start it deserves. For an extra pinch of flavor, use tomatoes that have been preserved in a mixture of olive oil and Italian herbs.

Ingredients (1 serving):

2 eggs, lightly beaten

25g feta cheese, crumbled

4 semi-dried tomatoes, roughly chopped

1 teaspoon olive oil

mixed salad leaves, for serving

Prep time: 5 min

Cooking time: 5 min

Preparation:

Heat the oil in a small, non-stick frying pan, then add the eggs and cook, swirling them with a wooden spoon. When the eggs are a bit runny in the middle, add the tomatoes and feta, then fold the omelet in half. Cook for 1 min, then slide it onto a plate and serve with a mix of leaf salad.

Nutritional value per serving: 300kcal, 18g protein, 20g fat (7 saturated), 5g carbs (1g fiber, 4g sugar), 1.8g salt, 15% calcium, 22% vitamin D, 20% vitamin A, 15% vitamin C, 25% vitamin B12.

2. Oatmeal with Apples and Raisins

A warm, filling, calcium rich breakfast that is easy on the stomach and perfect as a pre-workout meal, due to its high carb content. Sprinkle with some cinnamon for a sweet, woody fragrance.

Ingredients (2 servings):

50g oats

250ml low-fat milk

2 apples, peeled and diced

50g raisins

½ tablespoon honey

Prep time: 5min

Cooking time: 10 min

Preparation:

Bring the milk to a boil in a saucepan over medium heat and stir with the oats for 3 minutes. When the concoction becomes creamy, add the apples and the raisins and boil for another 2min. Ladle the mix into 2 bowls, add the honey and serve immediately.

Nutritional value per serving: 256kcal, 9g protein, 2g fat (1g saturated), 47g carbs (4g fiber, 34g sugar), 17% calcium, 11% iron, 17% magnesium.

3. Hummus with Pita Bread and Vegetables

This is a simple and nutritious breakfast that you can quickly assemble in the morning and pack to work. The hummus stays in the fridge and the vegetables can be stuffed into the pita bread, making an easy to grab sandwich.

Ingredients (2 servings):

1 200g can of chickpeas, drained

1 clove of garlic, crushed

25g of tahini

¼ teaspoon cumin

lemon juice, squeezed from ¼ lemon

salt, pepper

3 tablespoons water

2 whole wheat pita bread

200g vegetable mix (carrots, celery, cucumber)

Prep time: 15 min

No cooking

Preparation:

Combine chickpeas, garlic, tahini, cumin, lemon juice, salt, pepper and water in a food processor and pulse several times until the mix becomes creamy.

Serve with toasted pita bread and vegetable mix.

Nutritional value per serving: 239kcal, 9g protein, 9g fat (1g saturated), 28g carbs (6g fiber, 4g sugar), 1,1g salt, 27% iron, 23% magnesium, 14% vitamin B1.

4. Spring Onion and Turkey Wraps

What better way to use leftover turkey bits, than to make a quick delicious tortilla sandwich? Give yourself a treat that is high in protein, low in saturated fat and flavored with the zesty taste of basil.

Ingredients (2 servings):

130g cooked turkey (boiled or roasted), shredded

3 spring onions, shredded

1 chunk of cucumber, shredded

2 curly lettuce leaves

1 tablespoons light mayonnaise

1 tablespoon pesto

2 whole wheat flour tortillas

Prep time: 5mins

No cooking

Preparation:

Mix together the pesto and mayonnaise. Divide the turkey, spring onions, cucumber and lettuce leaves between the 2 tortillas. Drizzle over the pesto dressing, wrap everything up and serve.

Nutritional value per serving: 267kcal, 24g protein, 9g fat (2g saturated), 25g carbs (2g fiber, 3g sugar), 1.6g salt, 34% vitamin B3, 27% vitamin B6.

5. Berry Smoothie

What better way to get half a day's worth of calcium than with this creamy yogurt based meal? Add some fibers and make it even more nutritional, by saving half the berries from the blender and tipping them over when the smoothie is done.

Ingredients (2 servings):

450g frozen berries

450g low fat yogurt

100ml low fat milk

25g porridge oats

1 teaspoon honey (optional)

Prep time: 10 min

No cooking

Preparation:

Mix the berries, yogurt and milk in a food processor until smooth. Then add and stir the porridge oats and pour into 2 glasses. Serve with a bit of honey.

Nutritional value per serving: 234kcal, 16g protein, 2g fat (2g saturated), 36g carbs (14g sugar), 45% calcium, 11% magnesium, 18% vitamin B2, 21% vitamin B12.

6. Poached Eggs with Smoked Salmon and Spinach

A filling, high-protein breakfast that will give your day a very satisfying start. You will have no problem reaching your daily requirement of vitamin A and your heart will thank you for the hearty amount of omega-3 fatty acids.

Ingredients (1 serving):

2 eggs

100g spinach, chopped

50g smoked salmon

1 tablespoon white vinegar

a little butter for spreading

1 piece of whole wheat bread, toasted

Prep time: 5 min

Cooking time: 20 min

Preparation:

Heat a non-stick frying pan, add the spinach and stir for 2 min.

In order to poach the eggs, bring a pan of water to the boiling point, add the vinegar and then lower the heat so that the water is simmering. Stir the water until you have a slight whirlpool then slide the eggs one by one. Cook each for about 4 minutes then remove the egg with a slotted spoon.

Butter the piece of toast then put the spinach on it, the smoked salmon and the eggs. Season as needed and serve.

Nutritional value per serving: 349kcal, 31g protein, 19g fat (6g saturated), 13g carbs (4g fiber, 2g sugar), 3.6g salt, 23% iron, 23% magnesium, 197% vitamin A, 46% vitamin C, 21% vitamin D, 15% vitamin B6, 18% vitamin B12.

7. Bacon and Brie Omelette with Salad

A tasty omelette for those who prefer starting the day with a healthy filling of eggs and protein. Cut the omelette into wedges for a frittata look and savor with a salad instead of bread to cut back on the calories.

Ingredients (2 servings):

3 eggs, lightly beaten

100g smoked lardoons

50g brie, sliced

a small bunch of chives, chopped

1 tablespoon olive oil

½ teaspoon red wine vinegar

½ teaspoon Dijon mustard

½ cucumber, halved and deseeded

100g radishes, quartered

Prep time: 5 min

Cooking time 15 min

Preparation:

Heat 1 teaspoon in a small pan, add the lardoons and fry until crisp, then take it out of the pan and let it drain on kitchen paper.

Heat 1 teaspoon of the oil in a non-stick frying pan, then mix together the lardoons, eggs and some ground pepper. Pour into the frying pan and cook over low heat until it is almost done, then add the Brie and grill until it is set and golden.

Mix the remaining olive oil, vinegar, seasoning and mustard in a bowl and toss the radishes and cucumber. Serve alongside the omelette.

Nutritional value per serving: 395kcal, 25g protein, 31g fat (12g saturated), 3g carbs (2g fiber, 3g sugar), 2.2g salt, 10% vitamin A, 13% vitamin C, 15% vitamin D, 13% vitamin B12.

8. Fitness smoothie

A dairy-free vegan smoothie with pomegranate juice that will energize you for work or sustain your workout. You can add a tablespoon of ground flaxseeds for another 2g of fiber at the low cost of an extra 37kcal.

Ingredients (1 serving):

125ml soya milk

150ml pomegranate juice

30g tofu

1 large banana, cut into chunks

1 teaspoon honey

1 tablespoon almond

2 ice cubes

Prep time: 5 min

No cooking

Preparation:

Blend the soya milk and pomegranate juice with 2 ice cubes until the ice has broken down.

Add the banana, honey and tofu and blend until smooth, then pour the mix into a glass and sprinkle it with the flaked almonds.

Nutritional value per serving: 366kcal, 10g protein, 12g fat (1g saturated), 55g carbs (4g fiber, 50g sugar), 13% calcium, 11% iron, 15% magnesium, 14% vitamin C, 25% vitamin B6.

9. Tuna on Toast

A really quick, low calorie recipe that delivers a high amount of neuron protective B12. If you want an energy boost, spread the paste on a piece of whole wheat bread at about 120kcal per piece and serve with the bell pepper on the side.

Ingredients (4 servings):

2 cans of tuna in water (185g), half drained

3 hard-boiled eggs

1 spring onion, finely chopped

5 small pickles, diced

salt, pepper

4 bell peppers, halved, with the seeds cleaned

Prep time: 5 min

Cooking time: 10 min

Preparation:

Combine the tuna, eggs, spring onion, pickles and seasoning in a food processor and mix until smooth.

Fill the halves of the bell peppers with the composition and serve.

Nutritional value per serving: 240kcal, 23g protein, 8g fat (2g saturated), 4g carbs (1g fiber, 2g sugar), 14% magnesium, 47% vitamin A, 28% vitamin B6, 142% vitamin B12,.

10. Banana Oatmeal Pancakes

Enjoy this healthier version of pancakes that replaces plain flower with rolled oats. The banana makes for a subtle sugar substitute, but you can also spread 1 teaspoon of honey (23kcal per teaspoon) if you feel like it.

Ingredients (8 pancakes):

50g rolled oats

4 eggs, lightly beaten

2 bananas, cut into chunks

½ teaspoon cinnamon

1 teaspoon olive oil for each pancake

Prep time: 5 min

Cooking time: 30 min

Preparation:

Combine all the ingredients in a food processor. Heat a non-stick frying pan, add a teaspoon of oil and drop ¼ cup of mix into the pan. Cook on each size until the pancake become lightly brown.

Nutritional value per pancake: 135kcal, 4g protein, 13g fat (3g saturated), 10g carbs (1g fiber, 3g sugar).

11. Breakfast Guacamole

You can't miss with a meal that contains avocado. High in healthy fats and fiber, with a smooth texture and a flavor richly enhanced by a bit of lemon juice, this breakfast guacamole will energize you till lunch.

Ingredients (2 servings):

1 ripe avocado

1 large tomato, roughly chopped

1 spring onion, finely chopped

1 clove of garlic crushed

lemon juice, from ½ lemon

salt

ground black pepper

2 slices of whole wheat bread, toasted

Prep time: 5 min

No cooking

Preparation:

Slice the avocado in half, lengthwise, then scoop out the pulp with a spoon and put it into a large bowl. Mash it up with a fork. Pour the lemon juice over the pulp and add the chopped tomato, the spring onion and garlic. Season with salt and lots of black pepper. Mix it around, spread it on a piece of toast and serve immediately.

Nutritional value per serving: 280kcal, 9g protein, 13g fat (2g saturated), 30g carbs (9g fiber, 5g sugar), 10% iron, 17% magnesium, 14% vitamin A, 29% vitamin C, 17% vitamin B6.

12. Egg and Veggies Breakfast Bakes

An inventive, easy to make breakfast that bakes an egg instead of frying it, saving you a substantial amount of saturated fats. The eggs make it filling, while the veggies are not only tasty but also loaded with vitamin A and C.

Ingredients (1 serving):

2 large field mushrooms

2 medium-sized tomatoes, halved

100g spinach

2 eggs

1 garlic clove, thinly sliced

1 teaspoon olive oil

Prep time: 5 min

Cooking time: 30 min

Preparation:

Heat the oven to 200C fan/gas 6. Put in the tomatoes and mushrooms into an ovenproof dish. Add the garlic, drizzle the oil and seasoning and then bake for 10 min.

Put the spinach in a large pan then pour over a kettle of boiling water to wilt it. Squeeze out the excess water and then add the spinach to the dish. Make a little gap between the veggies and crack the eggs into the dish. Cook for another 10 min in the oven until the eggs are done.

Nutritional value per serving: 254kcal, 18g protein, 16g fat (4g saturated), 16g carbs (6g fiber, 10g sugar), 31% iron, 17% calcium, 29% magnesium, 238% vitamin A, 11% vitamin D, 102% vitamin C, 18% vitamin B1, 51% vitamin B2, 20% vitamin B3, 29% vitamin B6, 22% vitamin B12.

13.   Fruit and Nuts Yogurt

A great alternative to cereal, this high-carb breakfast will keep you full till lunch and give you the energy start you require to tackle your tasks. The mix of nuts delivers a substantial amount of healthy fats, while the yogurt makes sure that you get half a day's worth of calcium.

Ingredients (1 serving):

1 medium-sized banana, sliced

100g blueberries (fresh or frozen and defrosted)

20g walnuts

20g hazelnuts

10g raisins

200g fat free yogurt

Prep time: 5 min

No cooking

Preparation:

Mix the fruit with the nuts, layer up in a bowl with yogurt and serve.

Nutritional value per serving: 450kcal, 13g protein, 25g fat (2g saturated), 54g carbs (9g fiber, 32g sugar), 44% calcium, 16% magnesium, 30% vitamin C, 36% vitamin B6.

LUNCH

14.   Egg Drop Soup with Chicken and Noodles

A quick and easy to make dish, perfect for a midday meal. The noodles contain enough energy boosting carbs that will sustain your throughout the day and the meat is loaded with vitamin B.

Ingredients (2 servings):

1 skinless, boneless chicken breasts, diced

1 egg, beaten

0.6l chicken soup

1 spring onion, finely chopped

70g whole wheat noodles

70g frozen sweet corn, or baby corn, halved lengthways

lemon juice

¼ teaspoon sherry vinegar

Prep time: 10 min

Cooking time: 15 min

Preparation:

Place the chicken and the soup in a large pan and bring to a simmer for 5 min. The noodles are to be cooked following the instructions on the pack.

Add the corn and boil for 2 min. Stir the broth and while it is still churning, hold a fork over the pan and pour the eggs over the prongs in a slow stream. Stir again in the same direction and then take it off the heat. Add the lemon juice and the vinegar.

Drain the noodles and divide them between 2 bowls. Pour the broth, scatter with the chopped onions and serve.

Nutritional value per serving: 273kcal, 26g protein, 6g fat (1g saturated), 30g carbs (3g fiber, 2g sugar), 1g salt, 96% vitamin B3, 42% vitamin B6.

15. Chicken and Corn Salad

A paprika-spiced chicken, served with grilled sweet corn and fresh, crisp lettuce, makes for a healthy, speedy salad, with copious amounts of vitamin B. The garlic based dressing tops an already tasty meal.

Ingredients (2 servings):

2 small skinless chicken breasts

1 corn cob

2 little gem lettuces, quartered lengthways

½ cucumber, diced

1 garlic cloves, crushed

1 tablespoon olive oil

1 teaspoon paprika

lemon juice, from half a lemon

salad dressing (2 servings):

1 clove garlic, crushed

75ml curd milk

1 tablespoon white wine vinegar

Prep time: 20 min

Cooking time: 20 min

Preparation:

Cut the chicken breasts lengthways in half so you are left with 4 chicken strips. Mix the paprika, garlic, 1 teaspoon oil and lemon juice with some seasoning and marinate the chicken for at least 20 min.

Heat a pan, add the remaining oil and cook the chicken for 3-4 min on each side until it is cooked through. Brush over the remaining oil and griddle the corn for about 5 min or until lightly charred. Make sure to cook evenly. Remove the corn cobs and cut off the kernels.

Combine the ingredients for the dressing.

Mix the cucumber and lettuce, put the chicken and corn on top and drizzle the dressing.

Nutritional value per serving : 253kcal, 29g protein, 8g fat (1g saturated), 14g carbs (3g fiber, 6g sugar), 20% iron, 40% magnesium, 96% vitamin B3, 72% vitamin B6.

16. Lemon Spaghetti with Broccoli and Tuna

15 minutes is all you need to whip up this zesty fish pasta that packs a significant energy punch. The mix of spaghetti, tuna and vegetable make this an all-round nutritious dish.

Ingredients (2 servings):

180g whole wheat spaghetti

100g can tuna in oil, drained

125g broccoli, cut into florets

40g pitted green olives, quartered

1 tablespoon capers, drained

juice and zest from ½ lemon

1 teaspoon olive oil, plus extra for drizzling

Prep time: 5 min

Cooking time: 10 min

Preparation:

Boil the spaghetti according to the instructions on the pack. 6 min in, add the broccoli and boil for 4 min or more until both are tender.

Mix the olives, shallots, capers, tuna, lemon zest and juice in a big bowl. Drain the pasta and broccoli, add to the bowl, mix well with the olive oil and black pepper and serve.

Nutritional value per serving: 440kcal, 23g protein, 11g fat (2g saturated), 62g carbs (5g fiber, 4g sugar), 1.4g salt, 12% iron, 20% magnesium, 25% vitamin A, 50% vitamin B3, 25% vitamin B6, 90% vitamin B12.

17. Lemon-rubbed Barbecued Salmon

Rich in healthy fats, protein and B vitamins, salmon is a fish that definitely deserves a spot on you plate. Serve with a simple mix of tomato and green salad to savor the fine taste of this lemony meal.

Ingredients (2 servings):

2*150g boneless salmon fillets

juice and zest ½ lemon

10g fresh tarragon, finely chopped

1 garlic clove, finely chopped

1 tablespoon oil

Prep time: 5 min

Cooking time: 10 min

Preparation:

Stir the lemon zest and juice, garlic, tarragon and olive oil in a dish, season with salt and pepper and then add the salmon fillets. Rub the mixture on the fish, cover and set aside for 10 min.

Heat the grill to high, remove the salmon fillets from the marinade, put them on a baking shit and grill for 7-10 min. Served when the salmon is just cooked through.

Nutritional value per serving: 322kcal, 31g protein, 22g fat (4g saturated), 1g carbs, 12% vitamin B2, 30% vitamin B1, 60% vitamin B3, 45% vitamin B6, 79% vitamin B12.

18. Rice and Tomato Soup

A hearty main course, the rice and tomato soup is a great way to take advantage of the fresh and savory tomatoes available in summer. You can also serve it cold, for a refreshing effect.

Ingredients (2 servings):

70g brown rice

200g tomatoes, chopped

1 teaspoon tomato puree

1 spring onion, finely chopped

1 small carrot, finely chopped

½ celery stick, finely chopped

½ l vegetable stock made with 1 cube

1 teaspoon golden caster sugar

1 teaspoon vinegar

a few parsley leaves, chopped

a few drops of pesto, to serve (optional)

Prep time: 10 min

Cooking time: 35 min

Preparation:

Heat the oil in a large pan, add the carrot, celery and onion and cook on medium heat until softened. Add the vinegar and sugar, cook for 1 min and then stir through the tomato puree. Add the tomatoes, the vegetable stock and the brown rise, cover and simmer for 10 min.

Divide into 2 bowls, and sprinkle some parsley, season. Add pesto if wanted.

Nutritional value per serving: 213kcal, 6g protein, 3g fat (1g saturated), 39g carbs (4g fiber, 13g sugar), 1.6g salt, 16% vitamin A, 22% vitamin C.

19. Spinach and Dates Stuffed Chicken

High in protein, with a balanced amount of carbs and lots of vitamins, this healthy meal covers pretty much everything, from nutrients to taste. The date and spinach stuffing add a welcomed sweetness.

Ingredients (2 servings):

2 boneless and skinless chicken breasts

100g spinach, chopped

1 small onion, finely chopped

1 garlic clove, finely chopped

4 dates, finely chopped

1 tablespoon pomegranate juice or honey

1 teaspoon cumin

1 tablespoon olive oil

100g frozen green beans

Prep time: 10 min

Cooking time: 15 min.

Preparation:

Heat the oven to 200C fan/gas 6. Heat the oil in a non-stick pan, add the onion, garlic and a dash of salt and cook for 5 min before adding the dates, spinach and ½ of the cumin. Cook for another 1-2 min.

Cut the chicken breasts in half, lengthways, and leave a part intact so as to be able to open them like a book. Stuff the chicken breasts and put them in an oven pan, add the rest of the cumin and seasoning, sprinkle with the honey or pomegranate juice and bake for 20 min. Serve with the frozen green peas, slightly steamed.

Nutritional value per serving: 257kcal, 36g protein, 4g fat (1g saturated), 21g carbs (3g fiber), 17% iron, 23% magnesium, 97% vitamin A, 36% vitamin C, 96% vitamin B3, 49% vitamin B6.

20. Bean and Pepper Chili

A healthy vegetarian midday meal with a spicy kick, this dish is a great way of getting 1/2 – 1/3 of your daily required amount of fiber. You can serve topped on a small portion of boiled brown rice with around 170kcal added to your meal.

Ingredients (2 servings):

170g peppers, deseeded and sliced

200g can kidney beans in chili sauce

200g can black beans, drained

200g tomatoes, chopped

1 small onion, chopped

1 teaspoon cumin

1 teaspoon chili powder

1 teaspoon sweet smoked paprika

1 teaspoon olive oil

Prep time: 15 min

Cooking time: 30 min

Preparation:

Heat the oil in a large pan, add the onion and pepper and cook for 8-10 min until softened. Add the spices and cook for 1 min.

Tip the beans and tomatoes, bring to a boil and simmer for 15 min. When the chili has thickened season and serve.

Nutritional value per serving: 183kcal, 11g protein, 5g fat (1g saturated), 26g carbs (12g fiber, 12g sugar), 16% iron, 14% magnesium, 16% vitamin A, 22% vitamin C, 14% vitamin B1.

21. Garlic Beef

Enjoy a quickly made beef steak that is not only high in protein and low in fat and carbs, but also loaded with vitamin B. Pair it with some cherry tomatoes for a filling and refreshing meal.

Ingredients (2 servings):

300g well-trimmed beef skirt

3 garlic cloves

2 tablespoons red wine vinegar

1 teaspoon black peppercorn

200g cherry tomatoes, halved with a splash of vinegar

Prep time: 10 min

Cooking time: 15min

Preparation:

Crush the peppercorns and garlic with a pinch of salt in a pestle and mortar until you have a slightly smooth paste, then stir in the vinegar. Sit the beef in dish, then rub the paste all over. Leave in the fridge for 2 hours.

Place a griddle pan over a very hot heat. Rub the marinade off the meat, add more salt. Cook the meat for about 5 min until charred on each side (make sure the cut is not too thick). Lift the meat onto a chopping board, then rest for 5 min before carving it into slices. Serve with cherry tomatoes.

Nutritional value per serving: 223kcal, 34g protein, 6g fats, 7g carbs (1g fiber, 3g sugar), 22% iron, 16% vitamin A, 22% vitamin C, 27% vitamin B2, 42% vitamin B3, 30% vitamin B6, 64% vitamin B12.

22. Grilled Fish with Moroccan Spiced Tomatoes

A sea bream based meal makes for an excellent source of protein. The South African sauce with its aromatic spices compliments its taste and it also goes well with sardines and sea bass.

Ingredients (2 servings):

2*140g skinless sea bream fillets

3 large tomatoes

1 ½ large red peppers, deseeded and halved

2 garlic cloves, crushed

20ml olive oil

1 teaspoon cumin

1 teaspoon ground paprika

1/8 teaspoon black pepper

a pinch of cayenne

small bunch parsley, roughly chopped

small bunch coriander, roughly chopped

Prep time: 30 min

Cooking time: 15 min

Preparation:

Heat the grill to high, place the peppers skin side up on a baking tray and place under the grill until black and blistered. Place in a bowl covered tightly and let them cool. When they are cool, remove the burnt skins then cut them into small pieces.

Skin the tomatoes, then cut into quarters, discard the seeds and dice.

Heat the oil in a large pan, add the garlic, the ground pepper and the spices and cook for 2 min. Add the peppers and tomatoes and cook over medium heat until the tomatoes are very soft. Smash the soft tomatoes and continue cooking until the liquid is reduced to sauce.

Heat the grill to high, place the fish on a baking tray lined with lightly oiled foil. Season and grill for 4-5 min until cooked through. Divide the sauce between plates place the fish on top and serve with the chopped herbs.

Nutritional value per serving: 308kcal, 25g protein, 18g fat (2g saturated), 16g carbs (4g fiber, 12 g sugar), 23%

magnesium, 45% vitamin A, 55% vitamin C, 12% vitamin B1, 12% vitamin B2, 14% vitamin B3, 34% vitamin B6.

23. Prawn Curry

You only need 20 min to make this delicious, curry flavored seafood dish. The creamy, aromatic cherry sauce goes very well with a serving of boiled brown rice at about 175kcal per serving.

Ingredients (2 servings):

200g raw frozen prawns

200g chopped tomatoes

25g sachet coconut cream

1 small onion, chopped

1 teaspoon Thai red curry paste

½ teaspoon fresh ginger root

1 teaspoon olive oil

coriander, chopped

Prep time: 5 min

Cooking time: 15 min

Preparation:

Heat the oil in a saucepan. Tip in the onion and ginger and cook for a few minutes until softened. Add the curry paste, stir and cook for 1 more min. Pour over the tomatoes and coconut cream, bring to boil and leave to simmer for 5 min, adding a little boiling water if the concoction gets too thick.

Add the prawns and cook for another 5-10 min. Sprinkle with the chopped coriander and serve.

Nutritional value per serving: 180kcal, 20g protein, 9g fat (4g saturated), 6g carbs (1g fiber, 5g sugar), 1g salt, 18% iron, 10% magnesium, 20% vitamin A, 26% vitamin C, 13% vitamin B3, 25% vitamin B12.

24. Chicken with Mushrooms

A healthy dish, this chicken casserole has a high amount of protein that will keep you full until dinner. The chicken thighs add extra flavor and juiciness, while the mushrooms are responsible for the tangy feel of this low calories midday meal.

Ingredients (2 servings):

250g boneless, skinless chicken thighs

125ml chicken stock

25g frozen peas

150g mushrooms

25g cubetti di pancetta

1 large shallot, chopped

1 tablespoon olive oil

1 teaspoon white wine vinegar

flour, for dusting

small handful parsley, finely chopped

Prep time: 15 min

Cooking time: 25 min

Preparation:

Heat 1 teaspoon of oil in a non-stick frying pan, season and dust the chicken with the flour. Brown on all sides then remove the chicken and fry the pancetta and mushrooms until softened.

And the rest of the olive oil and cook the shallots for 5 min. Add the stock, the vinegar and bubble for 1-2 min. Return the chicken, pancetta and mushrooms to the pan and cook for 15 min. Add the peas and parsley, cook for 2 more minutes, then serve.

Nutritional value per serving: 260kcal, 32g protein, 13g fat (3g saturated), 4g carbs (3g fiber, 1 g sugar), 1g salt, 21% iron, 39% vitamin D, 12% vitamin B2, 34% vitamin B3, 17% vitamin B6.

25. Turkey Stir Fry

High in protein, quickly made and flavorsome, this dish is a perfect, spicy lunch. Its carbs content will load you with energy so it can also be an ideal pre-workout meal.

Ingredients (2 servings):

200g turkey breast steaks, cut into strips (remove fat)

150g rice noodles

170g green beans, halved

1 garlic clove, sliced

1 small red onion, sliced

½ red chili, finely chopped

juice from ½ lime

½ teaspoon olive oil

½ teaspoon chili powder

1 teaspoon fish sauce

Mint, roughly chopped

Coriander, roughly chopped

Prep time: 10 min

Cooking time: 15 min

Preparation:

Cook the noodles following the instructions on the pack. Heat the oil in a non-stick pan and fry the turkey over a high heat for 2 min. Add the onion, garlic and beans and cook for another 5 min.

Tip over the lime juice, fresh chili, chili powder and fish sauce, stir and cook for 3 min. Stir in the noodles and herbs according to taste and serve.

Nutritional value per serving: 425kcal, 32g protein, 3g fat (1g saturated), 71g carbs (4g fiber, 4g sugar), 1 g salt, 12% iron, 10% magnesium, 12% vitamin A, 36% vitamin C, 13% vitamin B1, 24% vitamin B2.

26. Tangy Trout

Try this easy, healthy trout recipe for a light summer meal. A great source of vitamin B12, this lemony white fish can be served with a side of green salad sprinkled with sea salt and a bit of lemon juice for an extra zesty feel.

Ingredients (2 servings):

2 trout fillets

15g pine nuts, toasted and roughly chopped

25g breadcrumbs

1 teaspoon soft butter

1 teaspoon olive oil

juice and zest from ½ lemon

1 small bunch of parsley, chopped

Prep time: 10 min

Cooking time: 5 min

Preparation:

Heat the grill to high. Lay the fillets, skin side down on an oiled baking tray.

Mix the breadcrumbs, lemon juice and zest, butter, parsley and half the pine nuts. Scatter the composition in a thin layer over the fillets, drizzle with the oil and place under the grill for 5 min. Sprinkle over the rest of the pine nuts and serve with steamed cauliflower or green beans.

Nutritional value per serving: 298kcal, 30g protein, 16g fat (4g saturated), 10g carbs (1g fiber, 1g sugar), 11% magnesium, 14% vitamin B1, 41% vitamin B3, 25% vitamin B6, 150% vitamin B12.

27. Spicy Seafood Stew

Treat your senses to this spicy mix of prawns, clams and white fish that delivers a hearty amount of protein and covers most of the B vitamins. Make sure to use fresh seafood to maximize the savory taste of this one-pot casserole.

Ingredients (2 servings):

100g large peeled raw prawns

150g clams

150g white fish fillets (cut into 3 cm pieces)

250g small new potatoes, halved and boiled

130g chopped tomatoes

350ml chicken stock

1 small onion, chopped

2 garlic cloves, chopped

1 dried ancho chili

juice from 1 lime

½ teaspoon smoked hot paprika

½ teaspoon ground cumin

1 teaspoon olive oil

lime wedges for serving (optional)

Prep time: 15 min

Cooking time: 30 min

Preparation:

Toast the chilies in a hot, dry frying pan until they puff up a bit, then remove, deseed and stem them. Soak in boiling water for 15 min.

Heat the olive oil in a large pan, add the onion, garlic and season and cook until softened. Add the paprika, chili, cumin, tomatoes and stock and sauté for 5 min, then puree in a blender until smooth. Pour back into the pan and bring to the boiling point. Let it simmer for 10 min. Add the prawns, fish fillets, clams and potatoes, place a lid on top of the pan and cook for 5 min over a medium-high heat. Serve with lime wedges if you like.

Nutritional value per serving: 347kcal, 44g protein, 6g fat (1 g saturated), 28g carbs (4g fiber, 7g sugar), 1.1g salt, 18% magnesium, 12% vitamin A, 40% vitamin C, 16%

vitamin B1, 10% vitamin B2, 23% vitamin B3, 26% vitamin B6, 62% vitamin B12.

DINNER

28. Stuffed Eggplant

A savory veggie meal, with a crisp cheese and breadcrumbs topping, that is light and perfect for dinner. Forget stuffed peppers and try this flavored eggplant instead.

Ingredients (2 serving):

1 eggplant

60g vegetarian mozzarella, torn into pieces

1 small onion, finely chopped

2 garlic cloves, finely chopped

1 tablespoon olive oil, plus extra for drizzling

2 garlic cloves, finely chopped

6 cherry tomatoes, cut in half

a handful of basil leaves, chopped

a few fresh whole eat breadcrumbs

Prep time: 15 min

Cooking time: 40 min

Preparation:

Heat the oven to 200C fan/gas 7. Slash the eggplant lengthways in half (you can leave the stem intact or remove it). Cut a border inside the eggplant about 1 cm thick. Using a teaspoon, scoop out the eggplant flesh until you are left with 2 shells. Chop the flesh then place it aside. Brush the shells with a little oil, season and place them in a baking dish. Cover it with a foil and bake for 20 min.

Add the remaining oil to a non-stick frying pan. Add the onion and cook until it is soft, then tip in the chopped eggplant flesh and cook through. Add the garlic and tomatoes and cook for another 3 min.

When the eggplant shells are tender, remove them from the oven, stuff them, sprinkle some breadcrumbs and drizzle with a little bit of oil. Reduce the heat in the oven to 180C fan/ gas 6. Bake for 15-20 min, until the cheese has melted and the breadcrumbs are golden. Serve with a green salad.

Nutritional value per serving: 266kcal, 9g protein, 20g fat (6g saturated), 14g carbs (5g fiber, 7g sugar), 1g salt, 15% vitamin A, 19% calcium.

29. Orange, Walnut and Blue Cheese Salad

Try this salty and sweet salad with crumbled blue cheese and chopped walnuts for a light supper. This, high in healthy fats and vitamin C, no cook recipe takes only 10 min to make and is a great way to end a busy day.

Ingredients (2 servings):

1*100g bag of bag of mixed salad (spinach, rocket and watercress)

1 large orange

40g walnuts, roughly chopped

70g blue cheese, crumbled

1 teaspoon walnut oil

Prep time: 10 min

No cooking

Preparation:

Empty the salad bag into a bowl. Peel the oranges and cut the segments from the pith over a small bowl to catch the juice. Whisk the walnut oil into the orange juice then pour over the salad leaves. Toss the salad, scatter over the orange segments, blue cheese and walnuts and serve.

Nutritional value per serving: 356kcal, 14g protein, 30g fat (10g saturated), 8g carbs (3g fiber, 8g sugar), 19% calcium, 10% magnesium, 20% vitamin A, 103% vitamin C, 10% vitamin B1.

30. Mexican Rice and Bean Salad

A low fat spicy meal with Latin American flavors, the Mexican rice and bean salad is packed with vegetables and makes for a filling supper. Tweak it a little and use a can of mixed beans for a more colorful plate.

Ingredients (2 servings):

90g brown rice

200g can black bean salad, drained

½ ripe avocado, chopped

2 spring onions, chopped

½ red pepper, deseeded and chopped

Juice from ½ lime

1 teaspoon Cajun spice mix

small bunch of coriander, chopped

Prep time: 15 min

Cooking time: 20 min

Preparation:

Cook the rice following the instructions on the pack. Drain then cool under running water until cold. Stir in the beans, pepper, onions and avocado.

Mix the lime juice with black pepper and the Cajun spices then pour over the rice. Add the coriander and serve.

Nutritional value per serving: 326kcal, 11g protein, 10g fat (2g saturated), 44g carbs (6g fiber, 4g sugar), 10% iron, 15% magnesium, 11% vitamin B1, 13% vitamin B6.

31. Chickpeas and Spinach Curry

Whip up this warming meal for a great night in. High in vitamin A and protein, this veggie dish can be served with a bit of Naan. Watch out for the extra calories though, one piece of Naan bread contains about 140kcal.

Ingredients (2 servings):

1*400g can chickpeas, drained

200g cherry tomatoes

130g baby spinach leaves

1 tablespoon curry paste

1 small onion, chopped

lemon juice

Prep time: 5 min

Cooking time: 15 min

Preparation:

Heat the curry paste in a non-stick frying pan. When it starts to split, add the onion and cook for 2 min until it softens. Tip in the tomatoes and bubble until the sauce has reduced.

Add the chickpeas and some seasoning and cook for an extra minute. Take off the heat, then tip the spinach (the heat of the pan will wilt the leaves). Season, add the lemon juice and serve.

Nutritional value per serving: 203kcal, 9g protein, 4g fat, 28g carbs (6g fiber, 5g sugar), 1.5g salt, 25% iron, 29% magnesium, 129% vitamin A, 61% vitamin C, 58% vitamin B6.

32. Thai Vegetable and Coconut Milk Broth

A serving of egg noodles topped with a delicious vegetable broth gives you a delectable and quick taste of Thai. If you prefer a thicker broth, use less vegetable stock, according to taste.

Ingredients (2 servings):

200ml can half-fat coconut milk

500ml vegetable stock

90g egg noodles

1 carrot, cut into matchsticks

¼ head Chinese leaf, sliced

75g beansprouts

3 cherry tomatoes, halved

2 small spring onions, halved and sliced lengthways

juice form ½ lime

1 ½ teaspoons Thai red curry paste

1 teaspoon brown sugar

1 teaspoon olive oil

handful coriander, roughly chopped

Prep time: 15 min

Cooking time 10 min

Preparation:

Heat the oil in a wok then add the curry paste and fry for 1 min until fragrant. Add the vegetable stock, brown sugar and coconut milk and simmer for 3 min.

Tip in the noodles, carrots and Chinese leaf and simmer until tender. Add the beansprouts and tomatoes, lime juice to taste and some extra seasoning. Spoon into bowls and sprinkle with coriander and spring onions.

Nutritional value: 338kcal, 10g protein, 14g fat (7g saturated), 46g carbs (5g fiber, 12g sugar), 1.2g salt, 14% iron, 16% magnesium, 10% vitamin B3.

33. Stuffed Zucchinis

A healthy veggie supper, light on the stomach and a delight to bake. The zucchinis are flavored by a mix of pine nuts, sundried tomatoes and fine parmesan cheese. You can brush the zucchinis with a bit of pesto instead of olive oil, before placing them in the oven.

Ingredients (2 servings):

2 zucchinis, halved lengthways

2 teaspoons olive oil

mixed salad, to serve

Stuffing:

25g pine nuts

3 spring onions, finely sliced

1 garlic clove, crushed

3 sundried tomatoes in oil, drained

12g parmesan, finely grated

25g dried white breadcrumbs

1 teaspoon thyme leaf

Prep time: 10 min

Cooking time: 35 min

Preparation:

Heat the oven to 200C fan/gas 7. Place the zucchinis in an ovenproof dish, cut-side up. Brush lightly with 1 teaspoon oil and bake for 20 min.

Mix all the stuffing ingredients together in a bowl and season with black pepper, sprinkle the mix on top of the zucchinis and drizzle with the remaining olive oil. Bake for another 10-15 min, until the zucchinis are softened and the topping is crisp. Serve hot with a mixed salad.

Nutritional value per serving: 244kcal, 10g protein, 17g fat (3 saturated), 14g carbs (3g fiber, 5g sugar), 56% vitamin C, 16% vitamin B2, 21% vitamin B6.

34. Fruit Salad

A vitamin C packed fruit salad sweetened with honey and ready to serve in 10 min. Make this simple fruit salad sing by adding a sprinkle of freshly-cut mint.

Ingredients (1 serving):

1 grapefruit, peel and pith cut away

2 apricots, sliced

2 oranges, peel and pith cut away

1 teaspoon clear honey

Prep time 5 min

No cooking

Preparation:

Put the apricots in a large bowl. Segment the oranges and grapefruits into the bowl to catch the juices. Stir in the honey and serve.

Nutritional value per serving: 166kcal, 4g protein, 36g carbs (8g fiber, 28g sugar), 46% vitamin A, 184% vitamin C, 13% vitamin B1.

35. Devilled Mushrooms

Treat yourself to a spicy, healthy meal, with a side of fresh, crisp salad. Double the serving for a higher fiber and protein content or pair it with a medium slice of baguette at about 150kcal per piece.

Ingredients (2 servings):

8 large flat mushrooms

2 garlic cloves, crushed

2 tablespoon olive oil

2 tablespoons Worcestershire sauce

2 tablespoons wholegrain mustard

1 teaspoon paprika

140g bag mixed salad leaves, with watercress and ruby chard

Prep time: 10 min

Cooking time: 15 min

Preparation:

Heat the oven to 180C fan/ gas 6. Mix together the mustard, oil, garlic and Worcestershire sauce in a large bowl, then season with freshly ground black pepper and salt. Add the mushrooms to the mix and toss well to coat them evenly. Place them stalk–side up in an ovenproof dish, sprinkle them with the paprika and bake for 8-10 min.

Divide the salad leaves between two serving plates with 4 mushrooms on each plate. Spoon over the juices and serve immediately.

Nutritional value per serving: 102kcal, 8g protein, 14g fat (2g saturated), 8g carbs (4g fiber), 1g salt, 20% vitamin B2, 16% vitamin B3.

36. Smoked Trout with Beetroot, Fennel and Apple Salad

A delicate hot-smoked fish complemented by a crisp apple and the colorful beetroot, makes for an exotic salad with a gorgeous flavor combination. Trout is an ideal source of B12 and high quality protein.

Ingredients (2 servings):

140g skinless smoked trout fillet

100g baby beetroot in vinegar, drained and quartered

4 spring onions, sliced

1 green-skinned apple, cored, quartered and sliced

½ small fennel bulb, trimmed and thinly sliced

small bunch dill leaves, finely chopped

2 tablespoons low-fat yogurt

1 teaspoon horseradish sauce

Prep time: 10 min

No cooking

Preparation:

Place the fennel in a serving dish and scatter over the beetroots, spring onions and apple. Cut the trout into chunky pieces and put on top. Sprinkle with half the dill.

Mix the yogurt and horseradish with 1 tablespoon cold water, then add the rest of the dill and stir. Pour half of the dressing over the salad and toss lightly, then spoon over the rest of the dressing and serve.

Nutritional value per serving: 183kcal, 19g protein, 5g fat (1g saturated), 16g carbs (5g fiber, 16g sugar), 1.6g salt, 12% iron, 11% vitamin A, 20% vitamin C, 20% vitamin B1, 17% vitamin B2, 20% vitamin B3, 100% vitamin B12.

37. Roasted Carrots with Pomegranate and Goat Cheese

An all-round full meal when it comes to nutrients, this combination of sweet vegetables and sour juices is a healthy and interesting dinner option. Make sure to keep the pomegranate seeds separate and add them just before serving if you plan on making a big batch.

Ingredients (2 servings):

375g carrots

40g pomegranate seeds

50g goat cheese, crumbled

200g can chickpeas, drained

grated zest and juice from ½ orange

1 tablespoon olive oil

1 teaspoon cumin seeds

small bunch mint, chopped

Prep time: 10 min

Cooking time: 50 min

Preparation:

Heat the oven to 170C fan/gas 5. Put the carrots in a bowl and toss with half the olive oil, the cumin seeds and orange zest and salt. Spread the carrots onto a large baking sheet and roast for 50 min until they get tender and catch some color on the edges.

Stir the chickpeas into the roasted carrots, then tip onto a serving platter. Drizzle with the remaining oil and the orange juice. Add the crumbled goat cheese, scatter with the pomegranate seeds and herbs and serve.

Nutritional value per serving: 285kcal, 12 g protein, 15g fat (6g saturated), 30g carbs (6g fiber, 16g sugar), 15% calcium, 12% iron, 14% magnesium, 610% vitamin A, 28% vitamin C, 12% vitamin B1, 18% vitamin B2, 11% vitamin B3, 37% vitamin B6.

38. Lentil, Carrot and Orange Soup

An interesting soup made with orange juice that will more than cover your daily required amount of vitamin C. Healthy, with flavors that work well together, this recipe is a spicy delight. You can thin it with some water if you find it too thick.

Ingredients (2 servings):

75g red lentils

225g carrots, diced

300ml orange juice

1 onion, chopped

600ml vegetable stock

2 tablespoons low-fat yogurt

1 teaspoon cumin seeds

2 teaspoons coriander seeds

freshly chopped coriander to garnish

Prep time: 15min

Cooking time: 35 min

Preparation:

Crush the seeds in a pestle and mortar, then dry-fry for 2 min until lightly browned. Add the lentils, carrots, onion, orange juice, stock and seasoning and bring to a boil. Cover and simmer for 30 min until the lentils have softened.

Transfer the mix to a food processor and blend until smooth. Return to the pan, reheat at medium heat and stir occasionally. Season to taste then ladle into bowls, swirl the yogurt over, sprinkle with the coriander leaves and serve at once.

Nutritional value per serving: 184kcal, 8g protein, 2g fat, 34g carbs (4g fiber), 1g salt, 340% vitamin A, 134% vitamin C, 16% vitamin B1, 11% vitamin B3, 13% vitamin B6.

39. Veggie Red Curry

It might take almost an hour to make, but this fragrant Thai dish will surely get your taste buds into action. Rich in nutrients, this creamy veggie curry has the makings of a standalone dish, but it can be also served with a side of boiled brown rice at around 175 extra kcal.

Ingredients (2 servings):

70g mushrooms, snapped

70g sugar snap peas

½ zucchini, chopped into chunks

½ eggplant, chopped into chunks

100g firm tofu, chopped into cubes

200ml can reduced-fat coconut milk

1 red chili (½ finely chopped, ½ sliced into rounds)

¼ red pepper, deseeded and chopped into chinks

2 tablespoons soy sauce

Juice from 1 lime

1 tablespoon olive oil

10g basil leaves

½ teaspoon brown sugar

Paste:

3 shallots, roughly chopped

2 small red chilies

½ lemongrass, roughly chopped

1 garlic cloves

stalks from 10g pack coriander

½ red pepper, deseeded and roughly chopped

zest form ½ lime

¼ teaspoon grated ginger root

½ teaspoon ground coriander

½ teaspoon freshly ground pepper

Prep time: 30 min

Cooking time: 20 min.

Preparation:

Marinate the tofu in half the lime juice, 1 tablespoon soy sauce and the chopped chili.

Place the paste ingredients in a food processor.

Heat half the oil in a pan, add 2 tablespoons of paste and fry for 2 min. Stir in the coconut milk with 50ml water, the eggplant, zucchini and pepper. Cook until almost tender.

Drain the tofu, pat it dry then fry it in the remaining oil in a small pan until golden.

Add the mushroom, sugar snaps and most of the basil, then season with the sugar, the rest of the lime juice and soy sauce. Cook until the mushrooms are tender, then add the tofu and heat through. Sprinkle with the basil, scatter the sliced chili and serve.

Nutritional value per serving: 233kcal, 8g protein, 18g fat (10g saturated), 11g carbs (3g fiber, 7g sugar), 3g salt, 13% calcium, 12% iron, 14% magnesium, 11% vitamin A, 65% vitamin C, 15% vitamin B1, 21% vitamin B2, 12% vitamin B3, 22% vitamin B6.

40. Mushroom Pilaf with Lemon

This low-fat mushroom pilaf is your ticket to a lighter alternative to risotto. Throw in a handful of green peas for a more colorful dish, and feel free to replace the chives with spring onions if you like.

Ingredients (2 servings):

100g brown rice

150g mushrooms, sliced

250ml vegetable stock

1 small onion, sliced

1 garlic clove, crushed

3 tablespoons light soft cheese with garlic and herbs

zest and juice from ½ lemon

small bunch of chives, snipped

Prep time: 10 min

Cooking time: 30 min

Preparation:

Place the onion in a non-stick pan, add a few tablespoons of the stock and cook for about 5 min until softened. Add the garlic and mushrooms and cook for 2 more minutes. While mixing, add the rice and lemon zest and juice. Pour in the remaining vegetable stock and seasoning and bring to a boil. Turn down the heat, cover the pan and let it simmer for 30 min until the rice is tender. Stir through half of each of the chives and soft cheese. Divide between 2 plates and serve topped with the remaining soft cheese and chives.

Nutritional value per serving : 249kcal, 12g protein, 4g fat (2g saturated), 44g carbs, 2g fiber, 4g sugar), 11% vitamin A, 23% vitamin B2.

OTHER GREAT TITLES BY THIS AUTHOR

Advanced Mental Toughness Training for Bodybuilders

Using Visualization to Push Yourself to the Limit

By

Joseph Correa

Certified Sports Nutritionist

Becoming Mentally Tougher in Bodybuilding by Using Meditation

Reach Your Potential by Controlling Your Inner Thoughts

By

Joseph Correa

Certified Sports Nutritionist

www.ingramcontent.com/pod-product-compliance
Lightning Source LLC
Chambersburg PA
CBHW071746080526
44588CB00013B/2170